THE
LOVE
OF
GOD

REV. DR. SUE PERRY

WESTBOW
PRESS®
A DIVISION OF THOMAS NELSON
& ZONDERVAN

WestBow Press books may be ordered through booksellers or by contacting:

WestBow Press
A Division of Thomas Nelson & Zondervan
1663 Liberty Drive
Bloomington, IN 47403
www.westbowpress.com
844-714-3454

All Scripture quotations are taken from King James version of the Bible, public domain.

ISBN: 979-8-3850-0891-9 (sc)
ISBN: 979-8-3850-0892-6 (e)

Library of Congress Control Number: 2023918600

Print information available on the last page.

WestBow Press rev. date: 10/10/2023

This book is dedicated to our Heavenly Father who gave all for us, Father, Son, and Holy Spirit.

God is love. (1John 4:8)

The vast, encompassing, unwavering, pure love of God is impossible to fully understand or even comprehend, yet it surrounds us, empowers us, and protects us.

We love him because he first loved us. (1 John 4:19)

Everything God does and has ever done is because of His love for us. The Bible is a love story written to and for God's people.

As we read His holy words, we see how He has proved His love repeatedly.

Let's start at what for us is the beginning. Although we will not see the manifest presence of His Son at first, know that He is always there, one with the Father.

In the beginning, God created the heaven and the earth. (Genesis 1:1)

He created the sun, the moon, and the stars, to give us light.

And God said, Let there be light: and there was light.
And God saw the light, that it was good: and God divided the light from the darkness.
And God called the light Day, and the darkness he called Night. And the evening and the morning were the first day. (Genesis 1:3–5)

He created the clouds, the earth, the sea, the mountains, and the valleys so that we could live in comfort and in beauty.

He gave us the sun to warm us, the breeze to cool us, and the night to rest us.

He created trees for food and beauty, the leaves of the trees for shade and comfort; and the ground to grow food.

> **And God said, Let the earth bring forth grass, the herb yielding seed, and the fruit tree yielding fruit after his kind, whose seed is in itself, upon the earth: and it was so.**
>
> **And the earth brought forth grass, and herb yielding seed after his kind, and the tree yielding fruit, whose seed was in itself, after his kind: and God saw that it was good. (Genesis 1:11–12)**

> **And God said, Behold, I have given you every herb bearing seed, which is upon the face of all the earth, and every tree, in the which is the fruit of a tree yielding seed; to you it shall be for meat. (Genesis 1:29)**

He created water for drinking and bathing and housing the fish of the sea.

> **And God created great whales, and every living creature that moveth, which the waters brought forth abundantly, after their kind, and every winged fowl after his kind: and God saw that it was good. (Genesis 1:21)**

He did it all for you and for me. Before we were born, God loved us so much that He created a perfect environment, a perfect abode for us to dwell in, an entire world.

Then He created us.

So God created man in his own image, in the image of God created he him; male and female created he them.

And God blessed them, and God said unto them, Be fruitful, and multiply, and replenish the earth, and subdue it: and have dominion over the fish of the sea, and over the fowl of the air, and over every living thing that moveth upon the earth. (Genesis 1:27–28)

That is love.

God made us in His image, gave us authority over every living creature, and called us His own!

Behold, what manner of love the Father hath bestowed upon us, that we should be called the sons of God. (1John 3:1)

Throughout the Bible, repeatedly, we see evidence of God's abundant love as He continued to create and deliver humanity.

Adam and Eve bore Cain and Able. Cain killed Able, and God knew Eve's pain. He gave her Seth and others.

Seth had sons and daughters who had sons and daughters and so forth, and Noah was born.

Humanity did not honor God in any way or form. It did not love Him and became exceedingly evil.

Yet, God did not destroy all of humankind. Rather, He preserved it through Noah and his family.

And the Lord said, I will destroy man whom I have created from the face of the earth; both man, and beast, and the creeping thing, and the fowls of the air; for it repenteth me that I have made them.

But Noah found grace in the eyes of the Lord.

These are the generations of Noah: Noah was a just man and perfect in his generations, and Noah walked with God.

And Noah begat three sons, Shem, Ham, and Japheth.

The earth also was corrupt before God, and the earth was filled with violence.

And God looked upon the earth, and, behold, it was corrupt; for all flesh had corrupted his way upon the earth.

And God said unto Noah, The end of all flesh is come before me; for the earth is filled with violence through them; and, behold, I will destroy them with the earth.

Make thee an ark of gopher wood; rooms shalt thou make in the ark, and shalt pitch it within and without with pitch.

And this is the fashion which thou shalt make it of: The length of the ark shall be three hundred cubits, the breadth of it fifty cubits, and the height of it thirty cubits.

A window shalt thou make to the ark, and in a cubit shalt thou finish it above; and the door of the ark shalt thou set in the side thereof; with lower, second, and third stories shalt thou make it.

And, behold, I, even I, do bring a flood of waters upon the earth, to destroy all flesh, wherein is the breath of life, from under heaven; and every thing that is in the earth shall die.

But with thee will I establish my covenant; and thou shalt come into the ark, thou, and

thy sons, and thy wife, and thy sons' wives
with thee.

And of every living thing of all flesh, two
of every sort shalt thou bring into the ark, to
keep them alive with thee; they shall be male
and female.

Of fowls after their kind, and of cattle after
their kind, of every creeping thing of the earth
after his kind, two of every sort shall come
unto thee, to keep them alive.

And take thou unto thee of all food that is
eaten, and thou shalt gather it to thee; and it
shall be for food for thee, and for them.

Thus did Noah; according to all that God
commanded him, so did he. (Genesis 6:7–22)

And the Lord said unto Noah, Come thou
and all thy house into the ark; for thee have I
seen righteous before me in this generation.
(Genesis 7:1)

And Noah went in, and his sons, and his
wife, and his sons' wives with him, into the ark,
because of the waters of the flood. (Genesis 7:7)

And it rained, and it rained, and it rained.

And the waters prevailed upon the earth an
hundred and fifty days. (Genesis 7:24)

Then at the appointed time, the waters receded, and the land
became dry.

And God remembered Noah, and every
living thing, and all the cattle that was with

him in the ark: and God made a wind to pass over the earth, and the waters assuaged. (Genesis 8:1)

And God spake unto Noah, saying,
Go forth of the ark, thou, and thy wife, and thy sons, and thy sons' wives with thee.
Bring forth with thee every living thing that is with thee, of all flesh, both of fowl, and of cattle, and of every creeping thing that creepeth upon the earth; that they may breed abundantly in the earth, and be fruitful, and multiply upon the earth.
And Noah went forth, and his sons, and his wife, and his sons' wives with him. (Genesis 8:15–18)

One wooden ark floated above the flood that cleansed the earth. And when the water subsided, one family and a lot of animals stepped out onto dry ground.

And God blessed Noah and his sons, and said unto them, Be fruitful, and multiply, and replenish the earth. (Genesis 9:1)

God showed His love as He provided a visual sign for Noah and all humanity.

And God spake unto Noah, and to his sons with him, saying,
And I, behold, I establish my covenant with you, and with your seed after you;
And with every living creature that is with you, of the fowl, of the cattle, and of every

beast of the earth with you; from all that go out of the ark, to every beast of the earth.

And I will establish my covenant with you, neither shall all flesh be cut off any more by the waters of a flood; neither shall there any more be a flood to destroy the earth.

And God said, This is the token of the covenant which I make between me and you and every living creature that is with you, for perpetual generations:

I do set my bow in the cloud, and it shall be for a token of a covenant between me and the earth.

And it shall come to pass, when I bring a cloud over the earth, that the bow shall be seen in the cloud:

And I will remember my covenant, which is between me and you and every living creature of all flesh; and the waters shall no more become a flood to destroy all flesh.

And the bow shall be in the cloud; and I will look upon it, that I may remember the everlasting covenant between God and every living creature of all flesh that is upon the earth.

And God said unto Noah, This is the token of the covenant, which I have established between me and all flesh that is upon the earth. (Genesis 9:8–17)

Every time we see a rainbow, we are reminded of God's love in living color. It brightens the sky and fills us with hope.

It is inconceivable to us that through one man an entire nation would evolve, yet that is exactly what happened.

And the sons of Noah, that went forth of the ark, were Shem, and Ham, and Japheth: and Ham is the father of Canaan.

These are the three sons of Noah: and of them was the whole earth overspread. (Genesis 9:18–19)

The Lord told Abraham to leave his country, his family, and go to a land He had chosen. He promised to bless Abram and make him a great nation, and He did.

It was not according to any plan of Abraham; it was according to God's perfect plan.

For my thoughts are not your thoughts, neither are your ways my ways, saith the Lord. (Isaiah 55:8)

"For I know the plans I have for you," declares the Lord, "plans to prosper you and not to harm you, plans to give you hope and a future." (Jeremiah 29:11)

Abraham and Sarah were well beyond child-bearing age and could not believe it when the angel of God told them they would have a son, but they did!

And the Lord visited Sarah as he had said, and the Lord did unto Sarah as he had spoken.

For Sarah conceived, and bare Abraham a son in his old age, at the set time of which God had spoken to him.

And Abraham called the name of his son that was born unto him, whom Sarah bare to him, Isaac.

> And Abraham circumcised his son Isaac being eight days old, as God had commanded him.
>
> And Abraham was an hundred years old, when his son Isaac was born unto him.
>
> And Sarah said, God hath made me to laugh, so that all that hear will laugh with me.
>
> And she said, Who would have said unto Abraham, that Sarah should have given children suck? for I have born him a son in his old age. (Genesis 21:1–7)

Abraham fathered Isaac.

Isaac fathered Jacob and Esau. There was jealousy, greed, and deception; however, God was in control.

Jacob had his issues, as we all do, which eventually led him to flee for his life. However, he was not alone. God was with him.

In a dream God spoke to Jacob saying,

> And, behold, the Lord stood above it, and said, I am the Lord God of Abraham thy father, and the God of Isaac: the land whereon thou liest, to thee will I give it, and to thy seed;
>
> And thy seed shall be as the dust of the earth, and thou shalt spread abroad to the west, and to the east, and to the north, and to the south: and in thee and in thy seed shall all the families of the earth be blessed.
>
> And, behold, I am with thee, and will keep thee in all places whither thou goest, and will bring thee again into this land; for I will not leave thee, until I have done that which I have spoken to thee of. (Genesis 28:13–15)

An encounter with the Lord! Jacob was a deceiver, but God loved him.

> **And Jacob vowed a vow, saying, If God will
> be with me, and will keep me in this way that I
> go, and will give me bread to eat, and raiment
> to put on,**
> **So that I come again to my father's house in
> peace; then shall the Lord be my God. (Genesis
> 28:20–21)**

God's love never fails.

Jacob fathered twelve sons, who became twelve tribes, who became a nation chosen and loved by God who brought forth the Savior.

When the people of God wandered from Him, He did not abandon them. God is faithful even when we are not.

When they became slaves, He was there. When they chose evil, God turned it to good.

Joseph was just one of Jacob's twelve sons, and when his brothers, through jealousy, sold him into slavery, it was unlikely that anyone other than his father mourned for him. As far as the world knew, "out of sight out of mind."

For Joseph, things seem to go from bad to worse. Purchased by the captain of the guards, things went well for a while as Joseph was placed in control of his master's household, but then he was betrayed by his captor's wife and thrown into prison. God was with him.

In prison, Joseph was blessed and blessed others, eventually, according to God's plan, becoming second to Pharaoh, which led to feeding multitudes of people, including his own family.

His brothers had thought to destroy Joseph, but the tables were turned when they were forced to go to him for food. After the death of their father, they feared for their lives. However,

> **And Joseph said unto them, Fear not: for
> am I in the place of God?**
> **But as for you, ye thought evil against me;
> but God meant it unto good, to bring to pass,**

as it is this day, to save much people alive.
(Genesis 50:19–20)

God hears our prayers and knows our need.

> And Joseph died, and all his brethren, and
> all that generation.
> And the children of Israel were fruitful,
> and increased abundantly, and multiplied, and
> waxed exceeding mighty; and the land was
> filled with them.
> Now there arose up a new king over Egypt,
> which knew not Joseph.
> And he said unto his people, Behold, the
> people of the children of Israel are more and
> mightier than we:
> Come on, let us deal wisely with them; lest
> they multiply, and it come to pass, that, when
> there falleth out any war, they join also unto
> our enemies, and fight against us, and so get
> them up out of the land.
> Therefore they did set over them taskmasters
> to afflict them with their burdens. And they
> built for Pharaoh treasure cities, Pithom and
> Raamses. (Exodus 1:6–11)

God saw the suffering of His people and because of His great love
for them, God called Moses, born of a Hebrew, raised by Pharaoh's
daughter, forced to flee Egypt, live in the desert of Midian for forty
years, a man of few words, humble in spirit, to lead His people out
of captivity. And he led the eventual exodus from Egypt through the
desert into the Holy Land—long ago promised to Abraham.

Throughout the Bible, we read of God's love as He continually
delivers His people, in spite of their refusal to obey Him; in ways we
never would have imagined.

God's love extends to all people. City walls crumbled at the sound of trumpets, and the harlot Rahab and her family were delivered.

> And Joshua the son of Nun sent out of Shittim two men to spy secretly, saying, Go view the land, even Jericho. And they went, and came into an harlot's house, named Rahab, and lodged there.
>
> And it was told the king of Jericho, saying, Behold, there came men in hither to night of the children of Israel to search out the country.
>
> And the king of Jericho sent unto Rahab, saying, Bring forth the men that are come to thee, which are entered into thine house: for they be come to search out all the country.
>
> And the woman took the two men, and hid them, and said thus, There came men unto me, but I wist not whence they were:
>
> And it came to pass about the time of shutting of the gate, when it was dark, that the men went out: whither the men went I wot not: pursue after them quickly; for ye shall overtake them.
>
> But she had brought them up to the roof of the house, and hid them with the stalks of flax, which she had laid in order upon the roof.
>
> And the men pursued after them the way to Jordan unto the fords: and as soon as they which pursued after them were gone out, they shut the gate.
>
> And before they were laid down, she came up unto them upon the roof;
>
> And she said unto the men, I know that the Lord hath given you the land, and that

THE LOVE OF GOD †|†

your terror is fallen upon us, and that all the inhabitants of the land faint because of you.

For we have heard how the Lord dried up the water of the Red sea for you, when ye came out of Egypt; and what ye did unto the two kings of the Amorites, that were on the other side Jordan, Sihon and Og, whom ye utterly destroyed.

And as soon as we had heard these things, our hearts did melt, neither did there remain any more courage in any man, because of you: for the Lord your God, he is God in heaven above, and in earth beneath.

Now therefore, I pray you, swear unto me by the Lord, since I have shewed you kindness, that ye will also shew kindness unto my father's house, and give me a true token:

And that ye will save alive my father, and my mother, and my brethren, and my sisters, and all that they have, and deliver our lives from death.

And the men answered her, Our life for yours, if ye utter not this our business. And it shall be, when the Lord hath given us the land, that we will deal kindly and truly with thee.

Then she let them down by a cord through the window: for her house was upon the town wall, and she dwelt upon the wall.

And she said unto them, Get you to the mountain, lest the pursuers meet you; and hide yourselves there three days, until the pursuers be returned: and afterward may ye go your way.

And the men said unto her, We will be blameless of this thine oath which thou hast made us swear.

Behold, when we come into the land, thou shalt bind this line of scarlet thread in the window which thou didst let us down by: and thou shalt bring thy father, and thy mother, and thy brethren, and all thy father's household, home unto thee.

And it shall be, that whosoever shall go out of the doors of thy house into the street, his blood shall be upon his head, and we will be guiltless: and whosoever shall be with thee in the house, his blood shall be on our head, if any hand be upon him.

And if thou utter this our business, then we will be quit of thine oath which thou hast made us to swear.

And she said, According unto your words, so be it. And she sent them away, and they departed: and she bound the scarlet line in the window. (Joshua 2:1–21)

God's love empowers His servants.

Now Jericho was straitly shut up because of the children of Israel: none went out, and none came in.

And the Lord said unto Joshua, See, I have given into thine hand Jericho, and the king thereof, and the mighty men of valour.

And ye shall compass the city, all ye men of war, and go round about the city once. Thus shalt thou do six days.

And seven priests shall bear before the ark seven trumpets of rams' horns: and the seventh day ye shall compass the city seven times, and the priests shall blow with the trumpets.

And it shall come to pass, that when they make a long blast with the ram's horn, and when ye hear the sound of the trumpet, all the people shall shout with a great shout; and the wall of the city shall fall down flat, and the people shall ascend up every man straight before him.

And Joshua the son of Nun called the priests, and said unto them, Take up the ark of the covenant, and let seven priests bear seven trumpets of rams' horns before the ark of the Lord.

And he said unto the people, Pass on, and compass the city, and let him that is armed pass on before the ark of the Lord.

And it came to pass, when Joshua had spoken unto the people, that the seven priests bearing the seven trumpets of rams' horns passed on before the Lord, and blew with the trumpets: and the ark of the covenant of the Lord followed them.

And the armed men went before the priests that blew with the trumpets, and the rereward came after the ark, the priests going on, and blowing with the trumpets.

And Joshua had commanded the people, saying, Ye shall not shout, nor make any noise with your voice, neither shall any word proceed out of your mouth, until the day I bid you shout; then shall ye shout.

So the ark of the Lord compassed the city, going about it once: and they came into the camp, and lodged in the camp.

And Joshua rose early in the morning, and the priests took up the ark of the Lord.

And seven priests bearing seven trumpets of rams' horns before the ark of the Lord went on continually, and blew with the trumpets: and the armed men went before them; but the rereward came after the ark of the Lord, the priests going on, and blowing with the trumpets.

And the second day they compassed the city once, and returned into the camp: so they did six days.

And it came to pass on the seventh day, that they rose early about the dawning of the day, and compassed the city after the same manner seven times: only on that day they compassed the city seven times.

And it came to pass at the seventh time, when the priests blew with the trumpets, Joshua said unto the people, Shout; for the Lord hath given you the city.

And the city shall be accursed, even it, and all that are therein, to the Lord: only Rahab the harlot shall live, she and all that are with her in the house, because she hid the messengers that we sent.

And ye, in any wise keep yourselves from the accursed thing, lest ye make yourselves accursed, when ye take of the accursed thing, and make the camp of Israel a curse, and trouble it.

But all the silver, and gold, and vessels of brass and iron, are consecrated unto the Lord: they shall come into the treasury of the Lord.

So the people shouted when the priests blew with the trumpets: and it came to pass, when the people heard the sound of the trumpet, and the people shouted with a great shout, that the wall fell down flat, so that the people went up into the city, every man straight before him, and they took the city.

And they utterly destroyed all that was in the city, both man and woman, young and old, and ox, and sheep, and ass, with the edge of the sword.

But Joshua had said unto the two men that had spied out the country, Go into the harlot's house, and bring out thence the woman, and all that she hath, as ye sware unto her.

And the young men that were spies went in, and brought out Rahab, and her father, and her mother, and her brethren, and all that she had; and they brought out all her kindred, and left them without the camp of Israel. (Joshua 6:1–23)

Only God's love would cause ravens to feed his prophet, save a widow from starving, and resurrect a child.

And Elijah the Tishbite, who was of the inhabitants of Gilead, said unto Ahab, As the Lord God of Israel liveth, before whom I stand, there shall not be dew nor rain these years, but according to my word.

And the word of the Lord came unto him, saying,

Get thee hence, and turn thee eastward, and hide thyself by the brook Cherith, that is before Jordan.

And it shall be, that thou shalt drink of the brook; and I have commanded the ravens to feed thee there.

So he went and did according unto the word of the Lord: for he went and dwelt by the brook Cherith, that is before Jordan.

And the ravens brought him bread and flesh in the morning, and bread and flesh in the evening; and he drank of the brook.

And it came to pass after a while, that the brook dried up, because there had been no rain in the land.

And the word of the Lord came unto him, saying,

Arise, get thee to Zarephath, which belongeth to Zidon, and dwell there: behold, I have commanded a widow woman there to sustain thee.

So he arose and went to Zarephath. And when he came to the gate of the city, behold, the widow woman was there gathering of sticks: and he called to her, and said, Fetch me, I pray thee, a little water in a vessel, that I may drink.

And as she was going to fetch it, he called to her, and said, Bring me, I pray thee, a morsel of bread in thine hand.

And she said, As the Lord thy God liveth, I have not a cake, but an handful of meal in a barrel, and a little oil in a cruse: and, behold, I am gathering two sticks, that I may go in and dress it for me and my son, that we may eat it, and die.

And Elijah said unto her, Fear not; go and do as thou hast said: but make me thereof a little cake first, and bring it unto me, and after make for thee and for thy son.

For thus saith the Lord God of Israel, The barrel of meal shall not waste, neither shall the cruse of oil fail, until the day that the Lord sendeth rain upon the earth.

And she went and did according to the saying of Elijah: and she, and he, and her house, did eat many days.

And the barrel of meal wasted not, neither did the cruse of oil fail, according to the word of the Lord, which he spake by Elijah.

And it came to pass after these things, that the son of the woman, the mistress of the house, fell sick; and his sickness was so sore, that there was no breath left in him.

And she said unto Elijah, What have I to do with thee, O thou man of God? art thou come unto me to call my sin to remembrance, and to slay my son?

And he said unto her, Give me thy son. And he took him out of her bosom, and carried him up into a loft, where he abode, and laid him upon his own bed.

And he cried unto the Lord, and said, O Lord my God, hast thou also brought evil upon the widow with whom I sojourn, by slaying her son?

And he stretched himself upon the child three times, and cried unto the Lord, and said, O Lord my God, I pray thee, let this child's soul come into him again.

And the Lord heard the voice of Elijah; and the soul of the child came into him again, and he revived.

And Elijah took the child, and brought him down out of the chamber into the house, and delivered him unto his mother: and Elijah said, See, thy son liveth.

> And the woman said to Elijah, Now by this
> I know that thou art a man of God, and that
> the word of the Lord in thy mouth is truth. (1
> Kings 17:1–24)

Only the love of God would answer the prayers of a barren woman. Hannah was barren.

> Now there was a certain man of
> Ramathaimzophim, of mount Ephraim, and
> his name was Elkanah, the son of Jeroham, the
> son of Elihu, the son of Tohu, the son of Zuph,
> an Ephrathite:
> And he had two wives; the name of the
> one was Hannah, and the name of the other
> Peninnah: and Peninnah had children, but
> Hannah had no children.
> And this man went up out of his city yearly
> to worship and to sacrifice unto the Lord
> of hosts in Shiloh. And the two sons of Eli,
> Hophni and Phinehas, the priests of the Lord,
> were there.
> And when the time was that Elkanah
> offered, he gave to Peninnah his wife, and to
> all her sons and her daughters, portions:
> But unto Hannah he gave a worthy portion;
> for he loved Hannah: but the Lord had shut up
> her womb.
> And her adversary also provoked her sore,
> for to make her fret, because the Lord had shut
> up her womb.
> And as he did so year by year, when she went
> up to the house of the Lord, so she provoked
> her; therefore she wept, and did not eat.

Then said Elkanah her husband to her, Hannah, why weepest thou? and why eatest thou not? and why is thy heart grieved? am not I better to thee than ten sons?

So Hannah rose up after they had eaten in Shiloh, and after they had drunk. Now Eli the priest sat upon a seat by a post of the temple of the Lord.

And she was in bitterness of soul, and prayed unto the Lord, and wept sore.

And she vowed a vow, and said, O Lord of hosts, if thou wilt indeed look on the affliction of thine handmaid, and remember me, and not forget thine handmaid, but wilt give unto thine handmaid a man child, then I will give him unto the Lord all the days of his life, and there shall no razor come upon his head.

And it came to pass, as she continued praying before the Lord, that Eli marked her mouth.

Now Hannah, she spake in her heart; only her lips moved, but her voice was not heard: therefore Eli thought she had been drunken.

And Eli said unto her, How long wilt thou be drunken? put away thy wine from thee.

And Hannah answered and said, No, my lord, I am a woman of a sorrowful spirit: I have drunk neither wine nor strong drink, but have poured out my soul before the Lord.

Count not thine handmaid for a daughter of Belial: for out of the abundance of my complaint and grief have I spoken hitherto.

Then Eli answered and said, Go in peace: and the God of Israel grant thee thy petition that thou hast asked of him.

And she said, Let thine handmaid find grace in thy sight. So the woman went her way, and did eat, and her countenance was no more sad.

And they rose up in the morning early, and worshipped before the Lord, and returned, and came to their house to Ramah: and Elkanah knew Hannah his wife; and the Lord remembered her.

Wherefore it came to pass, when the time was come about after Hannah had conceived, that she bare a son, and called his name Samuel, saying, Because I have asked him of the Lord.

And the man Elkanah, and all his house, went up to offer unto the Lord the yearly sacrifice, and his vow.

But Hannah went not up; for she said unto her husband, I will not go up until the child be weaned, and then I will bring him, that he may appear before the Lord, and there abide for ever.

And Elkanah her husband said unto her, Do what seemeth thee good; tarry until thou have weaned him; only the Lord establish his word. So the woman abode, and gave her son suck until she weaned him.

And when she had weaned him, she took him up with her, with three bullocks, and one ephah of flour, and a bottle of wine, and brought him unto the house of the Lord in Shiloh: and the child was young.

And they slew a bullock, and brought the child to Eli.

And she said, Oh my lord, as thy soul liveth, my lord, I am the woman that stood by thee here, praying unto the Lord.

For this child I prayed; and the Lord hath given me my petition which I asked of him:

Therefore also I have lent him to the Lord; as long as he liveth he shall be lent to the Lord. And he worshipped the Lord there. (1 Samuel 1:1–28)

Hannah prayed for a son; vowing to give him to the Lord. God heard Hannah's prayers (as He does all of ours) and He gave her a son, Samuel.

That was not the end of the story. God's love is personal, and He calls us by name.

And the child Samuel ministered unto the Lord before Eli. And the word of the Lord was precious in those days; there was no open vision.

And it came to pass at that time, when Eli was laid down in his place, and his eyes began to wax dim, that he could not see;

And ere the lamp of God went out in the temple of the Lord, where the ark of God was, and Samuel was laid down to sleep;

That the Lord called Samuel: and he answered, Here am I.

And he ran unto Eli, and said, Here am I; for thou calledst me. And he said, I called not; lie down again. And he went and lay down.

And the Lord called yet again, Samuel. And Samuel arose and went to Eli, and said, Here am I; for thou didst call me. And he answered, I called not, my son; lie down again.

Now Samuel did not yet know the Lord, neither was the word of the Lord yet revealed unto him.

And the Lord called Samuel again the third time. And he arose and went to Eli, and said, Here am I; for thou didst call me. And Eli perceived that the Lord had called the child.

Therefore Eli said unto Samuel, Go, lie down: and it shall be, if he call thee, that thou shalt say, Speak, Lord; for thy servant heareth. So Samuel went and lay down in his place.

And the Lord came, and stood, and called as at other times, Samuel, Samuel. Then Samuel answered, Speak; for thy servant heareth. (1 Samuel 3:1–10)

God's love is active in the lives of His people.

And Samuel grew, and the Lord was with him, and did let none of his words fall to the ground.

And all Israel from Dan even to Beersheba knew that Samuel was established to be a prophet of the Lord. (1 Samuel 3:19–20)

Samuel became a mighty prophet of God, guiding his people. Even a lion is not stronger than the power of God's love.

It pleased Darius to set over the kingdom an hundred and twenty princes, which should be over the whole kingdom;

And over these three presidents; of whom Daniel was first: that the princes might give accounts unto them, and the king should have no damage.

Then this Daniel was preferred above the presidents and princes, because an excellent spirit was in him; and the king thought to set him over the whole realm.

Then the presidents and princes sought to find occasion against Daniel concerning the kingdom; but they could find none occasion nor fault; forasmuch as he was faithful, neither was there any error or fault found in him.

Then said these men, We shall not find any occasion against this Daniel, except we find it against him concerning the law of his God.

Then these presidents and princes assembled together to the king, and said thus unto him, King Darius, live for ever.

All the presidents of the kingdom, the governors, and the princes, the counsellors, and the captains, have consulted together to establish a royal statute, and to make a firm decree, that whosoever shall ask a petition of any God or man for thirty days, save of thee, O king, he shall be cast into the den of lions.

Now, O king, establish the decree, and sign the writing, that it be not changed, according to the law of the Medes and Persians, which altereth not.

Wherefore king Darius signed the writing and the decree.

Now when Daniel knew that the writing was signed, he went into his house; and his windows being open in his chamber toward Jerusalem, he kneeled upon his knees three times a day, and prayed, and gave thanks before his God, as he did aforetime.

Then these men assembled, and found Daniel praying and making supplication before his God.

Then they came near, and spake before the king concerning the king's decree; Hast thou not signed a decree, that every man that shall ask a petition of any God or man within thirty days, save of thee, O king, shall be cast into the den of lions? The king answered and said, The thing is true, according to the law of the Medes and Persians, which altereth not.

Then answered they and said before the king, That Daniel, which is of the children of the captivity of Judah, regardeth not thee, O king, nor the decree that thou hast signed, but maketh his petition three times a day.

Then the king, when he heard these words, was sore displeased with himself, and set his heart on Daniel to deliver him: and he laboured till the going down of the sun to deliver him.

Then these men assembled unto the king, and said unto the king, Know, O king, that the law of the Medes and Persians is, That no decree nor statute which the king establisheth may be changed.

Then the king commanded, and they brought Daniel, and cast him into the den of lions. Now the king spake and said unto Daniel, Thy God whom thou servest continually, he will deliver thee.

And a stone was brought, and laid upon the mouth of the den; and the king sealed it with his own signet, and with the signet of his lords; that the purpose might not be changed concerning Daniel.

Then the king went to his palace, and passed the night fasting: neither were instruments of musick brought before him: and his sleep went from him.

Then the king arose very early in the morning, and went in haste unto the den of lions.

And when he came to the den, he cried with a lamentable voice unto Daniel: and the king spake and said to Daniel, O Daniel, servant of the living God, is thy God, whom thou servest continually, able to deliver thee from the lions?

Then said Daniel unto the king, O king, live for ever.

My God hath sent his angel, and hath shut the lions' mouths, that they have not hurt me: forasmuch as before him innocency was found in me; and also before thee, O king, have I done no hurt.

Then was the king exceedingly glad for him, and commanded that they should take Daniel up out of the den. So Daniel was taken up out of the den, and no manner of hurt was found upon him, because he believed in his God.

And the king commanded, and they brought those men which had accused Daniel, and they cast them into the den of lions, them, their children, and their wives; and the lions had the mastery of them, and brake all their bones in pieces or ever they came at the bottom of the den.

Then king Darius wrote unto all people, nations, and languages, that dwell in all the earth; Peace be multiplied unto you.

I make a decree, That in every dominion of my kingdom men tremble and fear before the God of Daniel: for he is the living God, and stedfast for ever, and his kingdom that which shall not be destroyed, and his dominion shall be even unto the end.

He delivereth and rescueth, and he worketh signs and wonders in heaven and in earth, who hath delivered Daniel from the power of the lions.

So this Daniel prospered in the reign of Darius, and in the reign of Cyrus the Persian. (Daniel 6:1–28)

God's love protects His servants.

Nebuchadnezzar the king made an image of gold, whose height was threescore cubits, and the breadth thereof six cubits: he set it up in the plain of Dura, in the province of Babylon.

Then Nebuchadnezzar the king sent to gather together the princes, the governors, and the captains, the judges, the treasurers, the counsellors, the sheriffs, and all the rulers of the provinces, to come to the dedication of the image which Nebuchadnezzar the king had set up.

Then the princes, the governors, and captains, the judges, the treasurers, the counsellors, the sheriffs, and all the rulers of the provinces, were gathered together unto the dedication of the image that Nebuchadnezzar the king had set up; and they stood before the image that Nebuchadnezzar had set up.

Then an herald cried aloud, To you it is commanded, O people, nations, and languages,

That at what time ye hear the sound of the cornet, flute, harp, sackbut, psaltery, dulcimer, and all kinds of musick, ye fall down and worship the golden image that Nebuchadnezzar the king hath set up:

And whoso falleth not down and worshippeth shall the same hour be cast into the midst of a burning fiery furnace.

Therefore at that time, when all the people heard the sound of the cornet, flute, harp, sackbut, psaltery, and all kinds of musick, all the people, the nations, and the languages, fell down and worshipped the golden image that Nebuchadnezzar the king had set up.

Wherefore at that time certain Chaldeans came near, and accused the Jews.

They spake and said to the king Nebuchadnezzar, O king, live for ever.

Thou, O king, hast made a decree, that every man that shall hear the sound of the cornet, flute, harp, sackbut, psaltery, and dulcimer, and all kinds of musick, shall fall down and worship the golden image:

And whoso falleth not down and worshippeth, that he should be cast into the midst of a burning fiery furnace.

There are certain Jews whom thou hast set over the affairs of the province of Babylon, Shadrach, Meshach, and Abednego; these men, O king, have not regarded thee: they serve not thy gods, nor worship the golden image which thou hast set up.

Then Nebuchadnezzar in his rage and fury commanded to bring Shadrach, Meshach, and Abednego. Then they brought these men before the king.

Nebuchadnezzar spake and said unto them, Is it true, O Shadrach, Meshach, and Abednego, do not ye serve my gods, nor worship the golden image which I have set up?

Now if ye be ready that at what time ye hear the sound of the cornet, flute, harp, sackbut, psaltery, and dulcimer, and all kinds of musick, ye fall down and worship the image which I have made; well: but if ye worship not, ye shall be cast the same hour into the midst of a burning fiery furnace; and who is that God that shall deliver you out of my hands?

Shadrach, Meshach, and Abednego, answered and said to the king, O Nebuchadnezzar, we are not careful to answer thee in this matter.

If it be so, our God whom we serve is able to deliver us from the burning fiery furnace, and he will deliver us out of thine hand, O king.

But if not, be it known unto thee, O king, that we will not serve thy gods, nor worship the golden image which thou hast set up.

Then was Nebuchadnezzar full of fury, and the form of his visage was changed against Shadrach, Meshach, and Abednego: therefore he spake, and commanded that they should heat the furnace one seven times more than it was wont to be heated.

And he commanded the most mighty men that were in his army to bind Shadrach, Meshach, and Abednego, and to cast them into the burning fiery furnace.

Then these men were bound in their coats, their hosen, and their hats, and their other garments, and were cast into the midst of the burning fiery furnace.

Therefore because the king's commandment was urgent, and the furnace exceeding hot, the flames of the fire slew those men that took up Shadrach, Meshach, and Abednego.

And these three men, Shadrach, Meshach, and Abednego, fell down bound into the midst of the burning fiery furnace.

Then Nebuchadnezzar the king was astonished, and rose up in haste, and spake, and said unto his counsellors, Did not we cast three men bound into the midst of the fire? They answered and said unto the king, True, O king.

He answered and said, Lo, I see four men loose, walking in the midst of the fire, and they have no hurt; and the form of the fourth is like the Son of God.

Then Nebuchadnezzar came near to the mouth of the burning fiery furnace, and spake, and said, Shadrach, Meshach, and Abednego, ye servants of the most high God, come forth, and come hither. Then Shadrach, Meshach, and Abednego, came forth of the midst of the fire.

And the princes, governors, and captains, and the king's counsellors, being gathered together, saw these men, upon whose bodies the fire had no power, nor was an hair of their head singed, neither were their coats changed, nor the smell of fire had passed on them.

Then Nebuchadnezzar spake, and said, Blessed be the God of Shadrach, Meshach, and Abednego, who hath sent his angel, and delivered his servants that trusted in him, and

have changed the king's word, and yielded their
bodies, that they might not serve nor worship
any god, except their own God.

Therefore I make a decree, That every
people, nation, and language, which speak
any thing amiss against the God of Shadrach,
Meshach, and Abednego, shall be cut in pieces,
and their houses shall be made a dunghill:
because there is no other God that can deliver
after this sort.

Then the king promoted Shadrach,
Meshach, and Abednego, in the province of
Babylon. (Daniel 3:1–30)

Whoever heard of a boy slaying a giant with a slingshot and a
pebble?

Now the Philistines gathered together their
armies to battle, and were gathered together
at Shochoh, which belongeth to Judah, and
pitched between Shochoh and Azekah, in
Ephesdammim.

And Saul and the men of Israel were gathered
together, and pitched by the valley of Elah, and
set the battle in array against the Philistines.

And the Philistines stood on a mountain on
the one side, and Israel stood on a mountain on
the other side: and there was a valley between
them.

And there went out a champion out of the
camp of the Philistines, named Goliath, of
Gath, whose height was six cubits and a span.

And he had an helmet of brass upon his
head, and he was armed with a coat of mail;

and the weight of the coat was five thousand shekels of brass.

And he had greaves of brass upon his legs, and a target of brass between his shoulders.

And the staff of his spear was like a weaver's beam; and his spear's head weighed six hundred shekels of iron: and one bearing a shield went before him.

And he stood and cried unto the armies of Israel, and said unto them, Why are ye come out to set your battle in array? am not I a Philistine, and ye servants to Saul? choose you a man for you, and let him come down to me.

If he be able to fight with me, and to kill me, then will we be your servants: but if I prevail against him, and kill him, then shall ye be our servants, and serve us.

And the Philistine said, I defy the armies of Israel this day; give me a man, that we may fight together.

When Saul and all Israel heard those words of the Philistine, they were dismayed, and greatly afraid.

Now David was the son of that Ephrathite of Bethlehemjudah, whose name was Jesse; and he had eight sons: and the man went among men for an old man in the days of Saul.

And the three eldest sons of Jesse went and followed Saul to the battle: and the names of his three sons that went to the battle were Eliab the firstborn, and next unto him Abinadab, and the third Shammah.

And David was the youngest: and the three eldest followed Saul.

But David went and returned from Saul to feed his father's sheep at Bethlehem.

And the Philistine drew near morning and evening, and presented himself forty days.

And Jesse said unto David his son, Take now for thy brethren an ephah of this parched corn, and these ten loaves, and run to the camp of thy brethren;

And carry these ten cheeses unto the captain of their thousand, and look how thy brethren fare, and take their pledge.

Now Saul, and they, and all the men of Israel, were in the valley of Elah, fighting with the Philistines.

And David rose up early in the morning, and left the sheep with a keeper, and took, and went, as Jesse had commanded him; and he came to the trench, as the host was going forth to the fight, and shouted for the battle.

For Israel and the Philistines had put the battle in array, army against army.

And David left his carriage in the hand of the keeper of the carriage, and ran into the army, and came and saluted his brethren.

And as he talked with them, behold, there came up the champion, the Philistine of Gath, Goliath by name, out of the armies of the Philistines, and spake according to the same words: and David heard them.

And all the men of Israel, when they saw the man, fled from him, and were sore afraid.

And the men of Israel said, Have ye seen this man that is come up? surely to defy Israel is he come up: and it shall be, that the man who killeth him, the king will enrich him with great riches, and will give him his daughter, and make his father's house free in Israel.

And David spake to the men that stood by him, saying, What shall be done to the man that killeth this Philistine, and taketh away the reproach from Israel? for who is this uncircumcised Philistine, that he should defy the armies of the living God?

And the people answered him after this manner, saying, So shall it be done to the man that killeth him.

And Eliab his eldest brother heard when he spake unto the men; and Eliab's anger was kindled against David, and he said, Why camest thou down hither? and with whom hast thou left those few sheep in the wilderness? I know thy pride, and the naughtiness of thine heart; for thou art come down that thou mightest see the battle.

And David said, What have I now done? Is there not a cause?

And he turned from him toward another, and spake after the same manner: and the people answered him again after the former manner.

And when the words were heard which David spake, they rehearsed them before Saul: and he sent for him.

And David said to Saul, Let no man's heart fail because of him; thy servant will go and fight with this Philistine.

And Saul said to David, Thou art not able to go against this Philistine to fight with him: for thou art but a youth, and he a man of war from his youth.

And David said unto Saul, Thy servant kept his father's sheep, and there came a lion, and a bear, and took a lamb out of the flock:

And I went out after him, and smote him, and delivered it out of his mouth: and when he arose against me, I caught him by his beard, and smote him, and slew him.

Thy servant slew both the lion and the bear: and this uncircumcised Philistine shall be as one of them, seeing he hath defied the armies of the living God.

David said moreover, The Lord that delivered me out of the paw of the lion, and out of the paw of the bear, he will deliver me out of the hand of this Philistine. And Saul said unto David, Go, and the Lord be with thee.

And Saul armed David with his armour, and he put an helmet of brass upon his head; also he armed him with a coat of mail.

And David girded his sword upon his armour, and he assayed to go; for he had not proved it. And David said unto Saul, I cannot go with these; for I have not proved them. And David put them off him.

And he took his staff in his hand, and chose him five smooth stones out of the brook, and put them in a shepherd's bag which he had, even in a scrip; and his sling was in his hand: and he drew near to the Philistine.

And the Philistine came on and drew near unto David; and the man that bare the shield went before him.

And when the Philistine looked about, and saw David, he disdained him: for he was but a youth, and ruddy, and of a fair countenance.

And the Philistine said unto David, Am I a dog, that thou comest to me with staves? And the Philistine cursed David by his gods.

And the Philistine said to David, Come to me, and I will give thy flesh unto the fowls of the air, and to the beasts of the field.

Then said David to the Philistine, Thou comest to me with a sword, and with a spear, and with a shield: but I come to thee in the name of the Lord of hosts, the God of the armies of Israel, whom thou hast defied.

This day will the Lord deliver thee into mine hand; and I will smite thee, and take thine head from thee; and I will give the carcases of the host of the Philistines this day unto the fowls of the air, and to the wild beasts of the earth; that all the earth may know that there is a God in Israel.

And all this assembly shall know that the Lord saveth not with sword and spear: for the battle is the Lord's, and he will give you into our hands.

And it came to pass, when the Philistine arose, and came, and drew nigh to meet David, that David hastened, and ran toward the army to meet the Philistine.

And David put his hand in his bag, and took thence a stone, and slang it, and smote the Philistine in his forehead, that the stone sunk into his forehead; and he fell upon his face to the earth.

So David prevailed over the Philistine with a sling and with a stone, and smote the Philistine, and slew him; but there was no sword in the hand of David. (1 Samuel 17:1–50)

Who would imagine a lowly shepherd boy becoming the king of Israel?

> And the Lord said unto Samuel, How long wilt thou mourn for Saul, seeing I have rejected him from reigning over Israel? fill thine horn with oil, and go, I will send thee to Jesse the Bethlehemite: for I have provided me a king among his sons.
>
> And Samuel said, How can I go? if Saul hear it, he will kill me. And the Lord said, Take an heifer with thee, and say, I am come to sacrifice to the Lord.
>
> And call Jesse to the sacrifice, and I will shew thee what thou shalt do: and thou shalt anoint unto me him whom I name unto thee.
>
> And Samuel did that which the Lord spake, and came to Bethlehem. And the elders of the town trembled at his coming, and said, Comest thou peaceably?
>
> And he said, Peaceably: I am come to sacrifice unto the Lord: sanctify yourselves, and come with me to the sacrifice. And he sanctified Jesse and his sons, and called them to the sacrifice.
>
> And it came to pass, when they were come, that he looked on Eliab, and said, Surely the Lord's anointed is before him.
>
> But the Lord said unto Samuel, Look not on his countenance, or on the height of his stature; because I have refused him: for the Lord seeth not as man seeth; for man looketh on the outward appearance, but the Lord looketh on the heart.

Then Jesse called Abinadab, and made him pass before Samuel. And he said, Neither hath the Lord chosen this.

Then Jesse made Shammah to pass by. And he said, Neither hath the Lord chosen this.

Again, Jesse made seven of his sons to pass before Samuel. And Samuel said unto Jesse, The Lord hath not chosen these.

And Samuel said unto Jesse, Are here all thy children? And he said, There remaineth yet the youngest, and, behold, he keepeth the sheep. And Samuel said unto Jesse, Send and fetch him: for we will not sit down till he come hither.

And he sent, and brought him in. Now he was ruddy, and withal of a beautiful countenance, and goodly to look to. And the Lord said, Arise, anoint him: for this is he.

Then Samuel took the horn of oil, and anointed him in the midst of his brethren: and the Spirit of the Lord came upon David from that day forward. (1 Samuel 16:1–13)

God's love looks within a person deep into the heart. David loved the Lord.

The love of God is always present. Throughout the Torah, the Writings, and the Prophets we see the continual love of God as He forgives His people delivering them time and again from their enemies, restoring them, providing leaders, warriors, judges, and others to free them from their oppressors.

Then God gave the ultimate gift of love, His Only Begotten Son, Jesus the Christ, and He used a simple maiden to bring Him forth.

And in the sixth month the angel Gabriel was sent from God unto a city of Galilee, named Nazareth,

To a virgin espoused to a man whose name was Joseph, of the house of David; and the virgin's name was Mary.

And the angel came in unto her, and said, Hail, thou that art highly favoured, the Lord is with thee: blessed art thou among women.

And when she saw him, she was troubled at his saying, and cast in her mind what manner of salutation this should be.

And the angel said unto her, Fear not, Mary: for thou hast found favour with God.

And, behold, thou shalt conceive in thy womb, and bring forth a son, and shalt call his name Jesus.

He shall be great, and shall be called the Son of the Highest: and the Lord God shall give unto him the throne of his father David:

And he shall reign over the house of Jacob for ever; and of his kingdom there shall be no end.

Then said Mary unto the angel, How shall this be, seeing I know not a man?

And the angel answered and said unto her, The Holy Ghost shall come upon thee, and the power of the Highest shall overshadow thee: therefore also that holy thing which shall be born of thee shall be called the Son of God.

And, behold, thy cousin Elisabeth, she hath also conceived a son in her old age: and this is the sixth month with her, who was called barren.

For with God nothing shall be impossible.

And Mary said, Behold the handmaid of the Lord; be it unto me according to thy word. And the angel departed from her. (Luke 1:26–38)

And it came to pass in those days, that there went out a decree from Caesar Augustus that all the world should be taxed.

(And this taxing was first made when Cyrenius was governor of Syria.)

And all went to be taxed, every one into his own city.

And Joseph also went up from Galilee, out of the city of Nazareth, into Judaea, unto the city of David, which is called Bethlehem; (because he was of the house and lineage of David:)

To be taxed with Mary his espoused wife, being great with child.

And so it was, that, while they were there, the days were accomplished that she should be delivered.

And she brought forth her firstborn son, and wrapped him in swaddling clothes, and laid him in a manger; because there was no room for them in the inn. (Luke 2:1–7)

Born in a lowly manger, loving the lowest of low, the Son of God lived that love every day of His life.

He called those whom others considered common to be His closest friends and disciples.

And he goeth up into a mountain, and calleth unto him whom he would: and they came unto him.

And he ordained twelve, that they should be with him, and that he might send them forth to preach,

And to have power to heal sicknesses, and to cast out devils:

And Simon he surnamed Peter;

And James the son of Zebedee, and John the brother of James; and he surnamed them Boanerges, which is, The sons of thunder:

And Andrew, and Philip, and Bartholomew, and Matthew, and Thomas, and James the son of Alphaeus, and Thaddaeus, and Simon the Canaanite,

And Judas Iscariot, which also betrayed him. (Mark 3:13–19)

He gave living water to a foreign woman; He showed no prejudice.

Then cometh he to a city of Samaria, which is called Sychar, near to the parcel of ground that Jacob gave to his son Joseph.

Now Jacob's well was there. Jesus therefore, being wearied with his journey, sat thus on the well: and it was about the sixth hour.

There cometh a woman of Samaria to draw water: Jesus saith unto her, Give me to drink.

(For his disciples were gone away unto the city to buy meat.)

Then saith the woman of Samaria unto him, How is it that thou, being a Jew, askest drink of me, which am a woman of Samaria? for the Jews have no dealings with the Samaritans.

Jesus answered and said unto her, If thou knewest the gift of God, and who it is that saith to thee, Give me to drink; thou wouldest have asked of him, and he would have given thee living water.

The woman saith unto him, Sir, thou hast nothing to draw with, and the well is deep: from whence then hast thou that living water?

Art thou greater than our father Jacob, which gave us the well, and drank thereof himself, and his children, and his cattle?

Jesus answered and said unto her, Whosoever drinketh of this water shall thirst again:

But whosoever drinketh of the water that I shall give him shall never thirst; but the water that I shall give him shall be in him a well of water springing up into everlasting life.

The woman saith unto him, Sir, give me this water, that I thirst not, neither come hither to draw.

Jesus saith unto her, Go, call thy husband, and come hither.

The woman answered and said, I have no husband. Jesus said unto her, Thou hast well said, I have no husband:

For thou hast had five husbands; and he whom thou now hast is not thy husband: in that saidst thou truly.

The woman saith unto him, Sir, I perceive that thou art a prophet.

Our fathers worshipped in this mountain; and ye say, that in Jerusalem is the place where men ought to worship.

Jesus saith unto her, Woman, believe me, the hour cometh, when ye shall neither in this mountain, nor yet at Jerusalem, worship the Father.

Ye worship ye know not what: we know what we worship: for salvation is of the Jews.

But the hour cometh, and now is, when the true worshippers shall worship the Father in spirit and in truth: for the Father seeketh such to worship him.

God is a Spirit: and they that worship him must worship him in spirit and in truth.

The woman saith unto him, I know that Messias cometh, which is called Christ: when he is come, he will tell us all things.

Jesus saith unto her, I that speak unto thee am he. (John 4:5–26)

He could have dined in a palace but chose to eat with sinners.

And as he passed by, he saw Levi the son of Alphaeus sitting at the receipt of custom, and said unto him, Follow me. And he arose and followed him.

And it came to pass, that, as Jesus sat at meat in his house, many publicans and sinners sat also together with Jesus and his disciples: for there were many, and they followed him.

And when the scribes and Pharisees saw him eat with publicans and sinners, they said unto his disciples, How is it that he eateth and drinketh with publicans and sinners?

When Jesus heard it, he saith unto them, They that are whole have no need of the physician, but they that are sick: I came not to call the righteous, but sinners to repentance. (Mark 2:14–17)

He openly chose to be with those others despised.

And Jesus entered and passed through Jericho.

And, behold, there was a man named Zacchaeus, which was the chief among the publicans, and he was rich.

And he sought to see Jesus who he was; and could not for the press, because he was little of stature.

And he ran before, and climbed up into a sycomore tree to see him: for he was to pass that way.

And when Jesus came to the place, he looked up, and saw him, and said unto him, Zacchaeus, make haste, and come down; for to day I must abide at thy house.

And he made haste, and came down, and received him joyfully.

And when they saw it, they all murmured, saying, That he was gone to be guest with a man that is a sinner.

And Zacchaeus stood, and said unto the Lord: Behold, Lord, the half of my goods I give to the poor; and if I have taken any thing from any man by false accusation, I restore him fourfold.

And Jesus said unto him, This day is salvation come to this house, forsomuch as he also is a son of Abraham.

For the Son of man is come to seek and to save that which was lost. (Luke 19:1–10)

He loves the little children.

Then were there brought unto him little children, that he should put his hands on them, and pray: and the disciples rebuked them.

But Jesus said, Suffer little children, and forbid them not, to come unto me: for of such is the kingdom of heaven. (Matthew 19:13–14)

He healed the sick and cleansed the leper.

When he was come down from the mountain, great multitudes followed him.

And, behold, there came a leper and worshipped him, saying, Lord, if thou wilt, thou canst make me clean.

And Jesus put forth his hand, and touched him, saying, I will; be thou clean. And immediately his leprosy was cleansed.

And Jesus saith unto him, See thou tell no man; but go thy way, shew thyself to the priest, and offer the gift that Moses commanded, for a testimony unto them.

And when Jesus was entered into Capernaum, there came unto him a centurion, beseeching him,

And saying, Lord, my servant lieth at home sick of the palsy, grievously tormented.

And Jesus saith unto him, I will come and heal him.

The centurion answered and said, Lord, I am not worthy that thou shouldest come under my roof: but speak the word only, and my servant shall be healed.

For I am a man under authority, having soldiers under me: and I say to this man, Go, and he goeth; and to another, Come, and he cometh; and to my servant, Do this, and he doeth it.

When Jesus heard it, he marvelled, and said to them that followed, Verily I say unto you, I have not found so great faith, no, not in Israel.

And I say unto you, That many shall come from the east and west, and shall sit down with Abraham, and Isaac, and Jacob, in the kingdom of heaven.

But the children of the kingdom shall be cast out into outer darkness: there shall be weeping and gnashing of teeth.

And Jesus said unto the centurion, Go thy way; and as thou hast believed, so be it done unto thee. And his servant was healed in the selfsame hour.

And when Jesus was come into Peter's house, he saw his wife's mother laid, and sick of a fever.

And he touched her hand, and the fever left her: and she arose, and ministered unto them.

When the even was come, they brought unto him many that were possessed with devils: and he cast out the spirits with his word, and healed all that were sick:

That it might be fulfilled which was spoken by Esaias the prophet, saying, Himself took our infirmities, and bare our sicknesses. (Matthew 8:1–17)

He caused the lame to walk, the blind to see, the mute to speak, and more.

And great multitudes came unto him, having with them those that were lame, blind,

47

dumb, maimed, and many others, and cast them down at Jesus' feet; and he healed them. (Matthew 15:30)

He fed the multitudes.

After these things Jesus went over the sea of Galilee, which is the sea of Tiberias.

And a great multitude followed him, because they saw his miracles which he did on them that were diseased.

And Jesus went up into a mountain, and there he sat with his disciples.

And the passover, a feast of the Jews, was nigh.

When Jesus then lifted up his eyes, and saw a great company come unto him, he saith unto Philip, Whence shall we buy bread, that these may eat?

And this he said to prove him: for he himself knew what he would do.

Philip answered him, Two hundred pennyworth of bread is not sufficient for them, that every one of them may take a little.

One of his disciples, Andrew, Simon Peter's brother, saith unto him,

There is a lad here, which hath five barley loaves, and two small fishes: but what are they among so many?

And Jesus said, Make the men sit down. Now there was much grass in the place. So the men sat down, in number about five thousand.

And Jesus took the loaves; and when he had given thanks, he distributed to the disciples, and the disciples to them that were set down;

and likewise of the fishes as much as they would.

When they were filled, he said unto his disciples, Gather up the fragments that remain, that nothing be lost.

Therefore they gathered them together, and filled twelve baskets with the fragments of the five barley loaves, which remained over and above unto them that had eaten. (John 6:1–13)

And,

Then Jesus called his disciples unto him, and said, I have compassion on the multitude, because they continue with me now three days, and have nothing to eat: and I will not send them away fasting, lest they faint in the way.

And his disciples say unto him, Whence should we have so much bread in the wilderness, as to fill so great a multitude?

And Jesus saith unto them, How many loaves have ye? And they said, Seven, and a few little fishes.

And he commanded the multitude to sit down on the ground.

And he took the seven loaves and the fishes, and gave thanks, and brake them, and gave to his disciples, and the disciples to the multitude.

And they did all eat, and were filled: and they took up of the broken meat that was left seven baskets full.

And they that did eat were four thousand men, beside women and children. (Matthew 15:32–38)

He is our sustenance.

> And Jesus said unto them, I am the bread of life: he that cometh to me shall never hunger; and he that believeth on me shall never thirst. (John 6:35)

He cast out demons.

> And they came over unto the other side of the sea, into the country of the Gadarenes.
>
> And when he was come out of the ship, immediately there met him out of the tombs a man with an unclean spirit,
>
> Who had his dwelling among the tombs; and no man could bind him, no, not with chains:
>
> Because that he had been often bound with fetters and chains, and the chains had been plucked asunder by him, and the fetters broken in pieces: neither could any man tame him.
>
> And always, night and day, he was in the mountains, and in the tombs, crying, and cutting himself with stones.
>
> But when he saw Jesus afar off, he ran and worshipped him,
>
> And cried with a loud voice, and said, What have I to do with thee, Jesus, thou Son of the most high God? I adjure thee by God, that thou torment me not.
>
> For he said unto him, Come out of the man, thou unclean spirit.
>
> And he asked him, What is thy name? And he answered, saying, My name is Legion: for we are many.

And he besought him much that he would not send them away out of the country.

Now there was there nigh unto the mountains a great herd of swine feeding.

And all the devils besought him, saying, Send us into the swine, that we may enter into them.

And forthwith Jesus gave them leave. And the unclean spirits went out, and entered into the swine: and the herd ran violently down a steep place into the sea, (they were about two thousand;) and were choked in the sea.

And they that fed the swine fled, and told it in the city, and in the country. And they went out to see what it was that was done.

And they come to Jesus, and see him that was possessed with the devil, and had the legion, sitting, and clothed, and in his right mind: and they were afraid. (Mark 5:1–15)

He had and still has compassion on those who grieve.

When Jesus therefore saw her weeping, and the Jews also weeping which came with her, he groaned in the spirit, and was troubled.

And said, Where have ye laid him? They said unto him, Lord, come and see.

Jesus wept. (John 11:33–35)

He taught us the two greatest commandments and how to love our neighbor.

And, behold, a certain lawyer stood up, and tempted him, saying, Master, what shall I do to inherit eternal life?

He said unto him, What is written in the law? how readest thou?

And he answering said, Thou shalt love the Lord thy God with all thy heart, and with all thy soul, and with all thy strength, and with all thy mind; and thy neighbour as thyself.

And he said unto him, Thou hast answered right: this do, and thou shalt live.

But he, willing to justify himself, said unto Jesus, And who is my neighbour?

And Jesus answering said, A certain man went down from Jerusalem to Jericho, and fell among thieves, which stripped him of his raiment, and wounded him, and departed, leaving him half dead.

And by chance there came down a certain priest that way: and when he saw him, he passed by on the other side.

And likewise a Levite, when he was at the place, came and looked on him, and passed by on the other side.

But a certain Samaritan, as he journeyed, came where he was: and when he saw him, he had compassion on him,

And went to him, and bound up his wounds, pouring in oil and wine, and set him on his own beast, and brought him to an inn, and took care of him.

And on the morrow when he departed, he took out two pence, and gave them to the host, and said unto him, Take care of him; and whatsoever thou spendest more, when I come again, I will repay thee.

Which now of these three, thinkest thou, was neighbour unto him that fell among the thieves?

And he said, He that shewed mercy on him. Then said Jesus unto him, Go, and do thou likewise. (Luke 10:25–37)

He raised the dead and healed a woman.

And it came to pass, that, when Jesus was returned, the people gladly received him: for they were all waiting for him.

And, behold, there came a man named Jairus, and he was a ruler of the synagogue: and he fell down at Jesus' feet, and besought him that he would come into his house:

For he had one only daughter, about twelve years of age, and she lay a dying. But as he went the people thronged him.

And a woman having an issue of blood twelve years, which had spent all her living upon physicians, neither could be healed of any,

Came behind him, and touched the border of his garment: and immediately her issue of blood stanched.

And Jesus said, Who touched me? When all denied, Peter and they that were with him said, Master, the multitude throng thee and press thee, and sayest thou, Who touched me?

And Jesus said, Somebody hath touched me: for I perceive that virtue is gone out of me.

And when the woman saw that she was not hid, she came trembling, and falling down before him, she declared unto him before all the people for what cause she had touched him, and how she was healed immediately.

And he said unto her, Daughter, be of good comfort: thy faith hath made thee whole; go in peace.

While he yet spake, there cometh one from the ruler of the synagogue's house, saying to him, Thy daughter is dead; trouble not the Master.

But when Jesus heard it, he answered him, saying, Fear not: believe only, and she shall be made whole.

And when he came into the house, he suffered no man to go in, save Peter, and James, and John, and the father and the mother of the maiden.

And all wept, and bewailed her: but he said, Weep not; she is not dead, but sleepeth.

And they laughed him to scorn, knowing that she was dead.

And he put them all out, and took her by the hand, and called, saying, Maid, arise.

And her spirit came again, and she arose straightway: and he commanded to give her meat.

And her parents were astonished: but he charged them that they should tell no man what was done. (Luke 8:40–56)

He taught the people how to live and love.

And when much people were gathered together, and were come to him out of every city, he spake by a parable:

A sower went out to sow his seed: and as he sowed, some fell by the way side; and it was trodden down, and the fowls of the air devoured it.

And some fell upon a rock; and as soon as it was sprung up, it withered away, because it lacked moisture.

And some fell among thorns; and the thorns sprang up with it, and choked it.

And other fell on good ground, and sprang up, and bare fruit an hundredfold. And when he had said these things, he cried, He that hath ears to hear, let him hear.

And his disciples asked him, saying, What might this parable be?

And he said, Unto you it is given to know the mysteries of the kingdom of God: but to others in parables; that seeing they might not see, and hearing they might not understand.

Now the parable is this: The seed is the word of God.

Those by the way side are they that hear; then cometh the devil, and taketh away the word out of their hearts, lest they should believe and be saved.

They on the rock are they, which, when they hear, receive the word with joy; and these have no root, which for a while believe, and in time of temptation fall away.

And that which fell among thorns are they, which, when they have heard, go forth, and are choked with cares and riches and pleasures of this life, and bring no fruit to perfection.

But that on the good ground are they, which in an honest and good heart, having heard the word, keep it, and bring forth fruit with patience.

No man, when he hath lighted a candle, covereth it with a vessel, or putteth it under a bed; but setteth it on a candlestick, that they which enter in may see the light.

For nothing is secret, that shall not be made manifest; neither any thing hid, that shall not be known and come abroad. (Luke 8:4–17)

Although a king, He washed the feet of His disciples.

Now before the feast of the passover, when Jesus knew that his hour was come that he should depart out of this world unto the Father, having loved his own which were in the world, he loved them unto the end.

And supper being ended, the devil having now put into the heart of Judas Iscariot, Simon's son, to betray him;

Jesus knowing that the Father had given all things into his hands, and that he was come from God, and went to God;

He riseth from supper, and laid aside his garments; and took a towel, and girded himself.

After that he poureth water into a bason, and began to wash the disciples' feet, and to wipe them with the towel wherewith he was girded.

Then cometh he to Simon Peter: and Peter saith unto him, Lord, dost thou wash my feet?

Jesus answered and said unto him, What I do thou knowest not now; but thou shalt know hereafter.

Peter saith unto him, Thou shalt never wash my feet. Jesus answered him, If I wash thee not, thou hast no part with me.

Simon Peter saith unto him, Lord, not my feet only, but also my hands and my head.

Jesus saith to him, He that is washed needeth not save to wash his feet, but is clean every whit: and ye are clean, but not all.

For he knew who should betray him; therefore said he, Ye are not all clean.

So after he had washed their feet, and had taken his garments, and was set down again, he said unto them, Know ye what I have done to you?

Ye call me Master and Lord: and ye say well; for so I am.

If I then, your Lord and Master, have washed your feet; ye also ought to wash one another's feet.

For I have given you an example, that ye should do as I have done to you.

Verily, verily, I say unto you, The servant is not greater than his lord; neither he that is sent greater than he that sent him.

If ye know these things, happy are ye if ye do them. (John 13:1–17)

He taught us to love.

A new commandment I give unto you, That ye love one another; as I have loved you, that ye also love one another.

By this shall all men know that ye are my disciples, if ye have love one to another. (John 13:34–35)

He gave His life for our lives; He paid the price of our sins.

He was oppressed, and he was afflicted, yet he opened not his mouth: he is brought as a lamb to the slaughter, and as a sheep before her shearers is dumb, so he openeth not his mouth. (Isaiah 53:7)

He went forth with his disciples over the brook Cedron, where was a garden, into the which he entered, and his disciples.

And Judas also, which betrayed him, knew the place: for Jesus ofttimes resorted thither with his disciples.

Judas then, having received a band of men and officers from the chief priests and Pharisees, cometh thither with lanterns and torches and weapons.

Jesus therefore, knowing all things that should come upon him, went forth, and said unto them, Whom seek ye?

They answered him, Jesus of Nazareth. Jesus saith unto them, I am he. And Judas also, which betrayed him, stood with them.

As soon then as he had said unto them, I am he, they went backward, and fell to the ground.

Then asked he them again, Whom seek ye? And they said, Jesus of Nazareth.

Jesus answered, I have told you that I am he: if therefore ye seek me, let these go their way:

That the saying might be fulfilled, which he spake, Of them which thou gavest me have I lost none.

Then Simon Peter having a sword drew it, and smote the high priest's servant, and cut off his right ear. The servant's name was Malchus.

Then said Jesus unto Peter, Put up thy sword into the sheath: the cup which my Father hath given me, shall I not drink it?

Then the band and the captain and officers of the Jews took Jesus, and bound him,

And led him away to Annas first; for he was father in law to Caiaphas, which was the high priest that same year.

Now Caiaphas was he, which gave counsel to the Jews, that it was expedient that one man should die for the people.

And Simon Peter followed Jesus, and so did another disciple: that disciple was known unto the high priest, and went in with Jesus into the palace of the high priest.

But Peter stood at the door without. Then went out that other disciple, which was known unto the high priest, and spake unto her that kept the door, and brought in Peter.

Then saith the damsel that kept the door unto Peter, Art not thou also one of this man's disciples? He saith, I am not.

And the servants and officers stood there, who had made a fire of coals; for it was cold: and they warmed themselves: and Peter stood with them, and warmed himself.

The high priest then asked Jesus of his disciples, and of his doctrine.

Jesus answered him, I spake openly to the world; I ever taught in the synagogue, and in the temple, whither the Jews always resort; and in secret have I said nothing.

Why askest thou me? ask them which heard me, what I have said unto them: behold, they know what I said.

And when he had thus spoken, one of the officers which stood by struck Jesus with the palm of his hand, saying, Answerest thou the high priest so?

Jesus answered him, If I have spoken evil, bear witness of the evil: but if well, why smitest thou me?

Now Annas had sent him bound unto Caiaphas the high priest.

And Simon Peter stood and warmed himself. They said therefore unto him, Art not thou also one of his disciples? He denied it, and said, I am not.

One of the servants of the high priest, being his kinsman whose ear Peter cut off, saith, Did not I see thee in the garden with him?

Peter then denied again: and immediately the cock crew.

Then led they Jesus from Caiaphas unto the hall of judgment: and it was early; and they themselves went not into the judgment hall, lest they should be defiled; but that they might eat the passover.

Pilate then went out unto them, and said, What accusation bring ye against this man?

They answered and said unto him, If he were not a malefactor, we would not have delivered him up unto thee.

Then said Pilate unto them, Take ye him, and judge him according to your law. The Jews therefore said unto him, It is not lawful for us to put any man to death:

That the saying of Jesus might be fulfilled, which he spake, signifying what death he should die.

Then Pilate entered into the judgment hall again, and called Jesus, and said unto him, Art thou the King of the Jews?

Jesus answered him, Sayest thou this thing of thyself, or did others tell it thee of me?

Pilate answered, Am I a Jew? Thine own nation and the chief priests have delivered thee unto me: what hast thou done?

Jesus answered, My kingdom is not of this world: if my kingdom were of this world, then would my servants fight, that I should not be delivered to the Jews: but now is my kingdom not from hence.

Pilate therefore said unto him, Art thou a king then? Jesus answered, Thou sayest that I am a king. To this end was I born, and for this cause came I into the world, that I should bear witness unto the truth. Every one that is of the truth heareth my voice.

Pilate saith unto him, What is truth? And when he had said this, he went out again unto the Jews, and saith unto them, I find in him no fault at all.

But ye have a custom, that I should release unto you one at the passover: will ye therefore that I release unto you the King of the Jews?

Then cried they all again, saying, Not this man, but Barabbas. Now Barabbas was a robber.

Then Pilate therefore took Jesus, and scourged him.

And the soldiers platted a crown of thorns, and put it on his head, and they put on him a purple robe,

And said, Hail, King of the Jews! and they smote him with their hands.

Pilate therefore went forth again, and saith unto them, Behold, I bring him forth to you, that ye may know that I find no fault in him.

Then came Jesus forth, wearing the crown of thorns, and the purple robe. And Pilate saith unto them, Behold the man!

When the chief priests therefore and officers saw him, they cried out, saying, Crucify him, crucify him. Pilate saith unto them, Take ye him, and crucify him: for I find no fault in him.

The Jews answered him, We have a law, and by our law he ought to die, because he made himself the Son of God.

When Pilate therefore heard that saying, he was the more afraid;

And went again into the judgment hall, and saith unto Jesus, Whence art thou? But Jesus gave him no answer.

Then saith Pilate unto him, Speakest thou not unto me? knowest thou not that I have power to crucify thee, and have power to release thee?

Jesus answered, Thou couldest have no power at all against me, except it were given thee from above: therefore he that delivered me unto thee hath the greater sin.

And from thenceforth Pilate sought to release him: but the Jews cried out, saying, If thou let this man go, thou art not Caesar's friend: whosoever maketh himself a king speaketh against Caesar.

When Pilate therefore heard that saying, he brought Jesus forth, and sat down in the judgment seat in a place that is called the Pavement, but in the Hebrew, Gabbatha.

And it was the preparation of the passover, and about the sixth hour: and he saith unto the Jews, Behold your King!

But they cried out, Away with him, away with him, crucify him. Pilate saith unto them, Shall I crucify your King? The chief priests answered, We have no king but Caesar.

Then delivered he him therefore unto them to be crucified. And they took Jesus, and led him away.

And he bearing his cross went forth into a place called the place of a skull, which is called in the Hebrew Golgotha:

Where they crucified him, and two other with him, on either side one, and Jesus in the midst.

And Pilate wrote a title, and put it on the cross. And the writing was Jesus Of Nazareth The King Of The Jews.

This title then read many of the Jews: for the place where Jesus was crucified was nigh to the city: and it was written in Hebrew, and Greek, and Latin.

Then said the chief priests of the Jews to Pilate, Write not, The King of the Jews; but that he said, I am King of the Jews.

Pilate answered, What I have written I have written.

Then the soldiers, when they had crucified Jesus, took his garments, and made four parts, to every soldier a part; and also his coat: now the coat was without seam, woven from the top throughout.

They said therefore among themselves, Let us not rend it, but cast lots for it, whose it shall be: that the scripture might be fulfilled, which saith, They parted my raiment among them, and for my vesture they did cast lots. These things therefore the soldiers did.

Now there stood by the cross of Jesus his mother, and his mother's sister, Mary the wife of Cleophas, and Mary Magdalene.

When Jesus therefore saw his mother, and the disciple standing by, whom he loved, he saith unto his mother, Woman, behold thy son!

Then saith he to the disciple, Behold thy mother! And from that hour that disciple took her unto his own home.

After this, Jesus knowing that all things were now accomplished, that the scripture might be fulfilled, saith, I thirst.

Now there was set a vessel full of vinegar: and they filled a spunge with vinegar, and put it upon hyssop, and put it to his mouth.

When Jesus therefore had received the vinegar, he said, It is finished: and he bowed his head, and gave up the ghost.

The Jews therefore, because it was the preparation, that the bodies should not remain upon the cross on the sabbath day, (for that sabbath day was an high day,) besought Pilate that their legs might be broken, and that they might be taken away.

Then came the soldiers, and brake the legs of the first, and of the other which was crucified with him.

But when they came to Jesus, and saw that he was dead already, they brake not his legs:

But one of the soldiers with a spear pierced his side, and forthwith came there out blood and water.

And he that saw it bare record, and his record is true: and he knoweth that he saith true, that ye might believe.

For these things were done, that the scripture should be fulfilled, A bone of him shall not be broken.

And again another scripture saith, They shall look on him whom they pierced.

And after this Joseph of Arimathaea, being a disciple of Jesus, but secretly for fear of the Jews, besought Pilate that he might take away the body of Jesus: and Pilate gave him leave. He came therefore, and took the body of Jesus.

And there came also Nicodemus, which at the first came to Jesus by night, and brought a mixture of myrrh and aloes, about an hundred pound weight.

Then took they the body of Jesus, and wound it in linen clothes with the spices, as the manner of the Jews is to bury.

Now in the place where he was crucified there was a garden; and in the garden a new sepulchre, wherein was never man yet laid.

There laid they Jesus therefore because of the Jews' preparation day; for the sepulchre was nigh at hand. (John 18:1–40, 19:1–42)

Nothing is stronger than the love of God, not even death. He arose! His love empowers those who believe.

> The first day of the week cometh Mary Magdalene early, when it was yet dark, unto the sepulchre, and seeth the stone taken away from the sepulchre.
>
> Then she runneth, and cometh to Simon Peter, and to the other disciple, whom Jesus loved, and saith unto them, They have taken away the Lord out of the sepulchre, and we know not where they have laid him.
>
> Peter therefore went forth, and that other disciple, and came to the sepulchre.
>
> So they ran both together: and the other disciple did outrun Peter, and came first to the sepulchre.
>
> And he stooping down, and looking in, saw the linen clothes lying; yet went he not in.
>
> Then cometh Simon Peter following him, and went into the sepulchre, and seeth the linen clothes lie,
>
> And the napkin, that was about his head, not lying with the linen clothes, but wrapped together in a place by itself.
>
> Then went in also that other disciple, which came first to the sepulchre, and he saw, and believed.
>
> For as yet they knew not the scripture, that he must rise again from the dead.
>
> Then the disciples went away again unto their own home.
>
> But Mary stood without at the sepulchre weeping: and as she wept, she stooped down, and looked into the sepulchre,

And seeth two angels in white sitting, the one at the head, and the other at the feet, where the body of Jesus had lain.

And they say unto her, Woman, why weepest thou? She saith unto them, Because they have taken away my Lord, and I know not where they have laid him.

And when she had thus said, she turned herself back, and saw Jesus standing, and knew not that it was Jesus.

Jesus saith unto her, Woman, why weepest thou? whom seekest thou? She, supposing him to be the gardener, saith unto him, Sir, if thou have borne him hence, tell me where thou hast laid him, and I will take him away.

Jesus saith unto her, Mary. She turned herself, and saith unto him, Rabboni; which is to say, Master.

Jesus saith unto her, Touch me not; for I am not yet ascended to my Father: but go to my brethren, and say unto them, I ascend unto my Father, and your Father; and to my God, and your God.

Mary Magdalene came and told the disciples that she had seen the Lord, and that he had spoken these things unto her.

Then the same day at evening, being the first day of the week, when the doors were shut where the disciples were assembled for fear of the Jews, came Jesus and stood in the midst, and saith unto them, Peace be unto you.

And when he had so said, he shewed unto them his hands and his side. Then were the disciples glad, when they saw the Lord.

> **Then said Jesus to them again, Peace be unto you: as my Father hath sent me, even so send I you.**
>
> **And when he had said this, he breathed on them, and saith unto them, Receive ye the Holy Ghost. (John 20:1–22)**

His love is what brings us peace for He is the Prince of Peace.

> **For unto us a child is born, unto us a son is given: and the government shall be upon his shoulder: and his name shall be called Wonderful, Counsellor, The mighty God, The everlasting Father, The Prince of Peace. (Isaiah 9:6)**

It is His love that upholds us.

> **The God of my rock; in him will I trust: he is my shield, and the horn of my salvation, my high tower, and my refuge, my saviour. (2 Samuel 22:3)**

His love is forever.

> **Let your conversation be without covetousness; and be content with such things as ye have: for he hath said, I will never leave thee, nor forsake thee. (Hebrews 13:5)**

Therefore, as the psalmist said,

> **I will sing of the mercies of the Lord for ever: with my mouth will I make known thy faithfulness to all generations. (Psalm 89:1)**

No matter the trouble, His love empowers us through His Holy Spirit.

> **What shall we then say to these things? If God be for us, who can be against us? (Romans 8:31)**

He calls us to Him. His love is tender and compassionate.

> **Come unto me, all ye that labour and are heavy laden, and I will give you rest.**
> **Take my yoke upon you, and learn of me; for I am meek and lowly in heart: and ye shall find rest unto your souls.**
> **For my yoke is easy, and my burden is light. (Matthew 11:28–30)**

That perfect love of God is from creation to eternity.

> **For God so loved the world, that he gave his only begotten Son, that whosoever believeth in him should not perish, but have everlasting life. (John 3:16)**

This and much more is the Love of God, and I know,

> **In all these things we are more than conquerors through him that loved us.**
> **For I am persuaded, that neither death, nor life, nor angels, nor principalities, nor powers, nor things present, nor things to come,**
> **Nor height, nor depth, nor any other creature, shall be able to separate us from the love of God, which is in Christ Jesus our Lord. (Romans 8:37–39)**

Finally, know that we have not been abandoned; our Lord will return for us.

For the Lord himself shall descend from heaven with a shout, with the voice of the archangel, and with the trump of God: and the dead in Christ shall rise. (1 Thessalonians 4:16)

The love of God was there at the beginning and has no end. There is nothing more powerful or faithful. It guides, protects, and delivers. It comforts and heals. It cannot be destroyed. It is free and empowers all who embrace it.

There is no greater love than the love of God, and you are His beloved.

You have been chosen to share His love and care for His people. Everything you have was given to you by God. Therefore, as the Apostle Paul said:

For this cause I bow my knees unto the Father of our Lord Jesus Christ,

Of whom the whole family in heaven and earth is named,

That he would grant you, according to the riches of his glory, to be strengthened with might by his Spirit in the inner man;

That Christ may dwell in your hearts by faith; that ye, being rooted and grounded in love,

May be able to comprehend with all saints what is the breadth, and length, and depth, and height;

And to know the love of Christ, which passeth knowledge, that ye might be filled with all the fulness of God.

Now unto him that is able to do exceeding abundantly above all that we ask or think, according to the power that worketh in us,

Unto him be glory in the church by Christ Jesus throughout all ages, world without end. Amen. (Ephesians 3:14–21)

God is love. Share the "Good News."

Printed in the United States
by Baker & Taylor Publisher Services